LAND OF
HUNTERS

CLIVE GIFFORD

Illustrated by
HOWARD GRAY

WELBECK

Published in 2023 by Welbeck Children's Books
An Imprint of Welbeck Children's Limited,
part of the Welbeck Publishing Group

OFFICES IN:
London—20 Mortimer Street, London W1T 3JW &
Sydney—Level 17, 207 Kent St. Sydney NSW 2000 Australia
www.welbeckpublishing.com

Consultant Paleontologist: Chris Barker
Editor: Gemma Farr
Design Manager: Matt Drew
Designer: Ceri Woods
Production: Melanie Robertson

A CIP record for
this book is available from the Library of Congress.

ISBN 978 1 78312 971 3

Printed in Heshan, China

10 9 8 7 6 5 4 3 2 1

CONTENTS

BEWARE: THE LAND OF HUNTERS

You're entering the world of the hunters. Tread carefully now...

All creatures need food to survive. Some specialize in plants, grazing, and browsing their way through their habitats. Meat, however, is often richer in energy. Some animals have adapted to take down others—these are nature's predators, creatures which hunt and eat other animals to survive.

Paleontologists—scientists who study prehistoric life—piece together fossils and other evidence to try to figure out precisely how predators hunted, fought, and survived in the past.

They may study the wear on teeth, the creature's jaw strength, or the size and position of claws to determine the sorts of creatures they ate. Exciting new discoveries are being made all the time. These help increase our knowledge of prehistoric hunters and how they captured their prey.

Among the most famous predators of the past are meat-eating dinosaurs like *Tyrannosaurus rex*, but the prehistoric world contained many, many more. Giant flying reptiles called pterosaurs would attack from the air or stalk prey on land. Flightless terror birds, taller than humans and armed with massive claws and beaks, hunted on the plains, and in Earth's waters were huge and hungry predators, some longer than buses.

Over millions of years, other hunters have evolved to take the place of those earlier predators. Some are still with us—from powerful big cats and agile sharks to swooping ospreys and dragonflies.

This book is packed with some of the most ferocious, stealthy, and terrifying hunters that have ever roamed the planet. Learn about their size, weapons, hunting techniques, and what they preyed on.

HUNTERS OF THE LAND

Dimetrodon (Di-met-ro-don) was a land-dwelling hunter that lived 286-270 million years ago— long before dinosaurs roamed the Earth. It had a giant sail on its back made of spines and webbed skin. Experts believe this may have been to attract mates. Several species of *Dimetrodon* are known to have evolved, with the largest being over 13ft long. The earlier species were smaller with smooth teeth. The later species were bigger and they evolved to have serrated teeth so they could take down larger prey with greater ease.

Deinonychus

This feathered dinosaur's name means "terrible claw" and with good reason. *Deinonychus* (Die-non-ick-us) sported a large 5in curved claw on the second toe of each foot. It wasn't the only weapon this prehistoric hunter owned; each of the three fingers were tipped with claws and its mouth was packed with 70 curved teeth.

Like *Velociraptor* (see p16), *Deinonychus* belonged to a family of two-legged dinosaurs called dromaeosaurs which means "running lizard." When they moved, they could lift that large toe-claw off the ground so it didn't get in their way. Scientists estimate that *Deinonychus* was around 11ft long, weighed 155-220lbs, and was a pretty agile mover. It may have used those deadly foot claws and its body weight to pin its prey down on the ground as it started to feed while its victim was still alive, a tactic used by some birds of prey today.

In the mid-1960s, a group of five fossilized *Deinonychus* were found surrounding the remains of a *Tenontosaurus* (Ten-on-toh-saw-rus) in the state of Montana. The find excited many scientists as possible evidence that some dinosaurs hunted together in packs to bring down dinosaurs much larger than themselves. However, it might also mean that a dead or dying *Tenontosaurus* attracted a number of *Deinonychus* as scavengers. For the moment, we cannot be sure.

What seems more certain is that *Deinonychus* did like dining out on *Tenontosaurus*—a plant-eating dinosaur weighing over a ton. We also think that it preyed on smaller dinosaurs such as baby or infant *Zephyrosaurus* (Zef-ee-ro-saw-rus) and possibly even other *Deinonychus*.

Riverbank Raiders

If you went down to the river 120 million years ago, you could be in for a terrifying surprise. At the time the continents of South America and Africa were one giant piece of land with large river systems. Two formidable hunters operated there, preying on fish, turtles, and dinosaurs.

SUCHOMIMUS 125-112 MYA

The name *Suchomimus* (Soo-ko-my-mus) means, "crocodile mimic." This two-legged dinosaur's skull was similar to a crocodile's with a long snout that housed 120 teeth. The rest of this type of spinosaurid, though, was quite different with two strong legs and two muscly arms. It would have towered over a person and measured around 36ft in length.

Suchomimus would have been expert at grabbing and grappling fish and small dinosaurs using its mouth. *Suchomimus* and other spinosaurs could snap their jaws shut at great speeds, perhaps helping them to catch agile prey.

SARCOSUCHUS 133-112 MYA

Large crocodiles today may reach up to 20ft in length. *Sarcosuchus* (Sar-ko-su-kus) grew to 31ft long and weighed up to 5 tons. It had a long, but relatively narrow skull which contained over 100 bulky teeth. Its body was covered with bony scales called osteoderms and its eye sockets were pointed a little upward. This would help it lie still as it looked up at the riverbank for prey to attack.

Palaeontologists have debated what this super-sized croc ate. Many think that large bony fish formed a major part of its diet. It may also have been capable of snaring creatures at the water's edge, possibly including large plant-eating dinosaurs of the time. Unlike modern crocs, *Sarcosuchus* would not have been able to perform a death roll—rolling over while gripping prey—for fear of breaking its own skull.

MEGAPIRANHA 9-7 MYA

Most piranha fish today weigh 2lb or less. *Megapiranha* may have weighed 22lb. This 28in-long predatory fish had oversized muscles working its stout jaw. These helped it bite and clamp down on prey with immense force. Relative to its size, it had one of the strongest bite-forces of any fish. This would have helped it crush through armoured defenses such as turtles' shells.

Tyrannosaurus rex 68-66 MYA

The infamous *Tyrannosaurus rex* (Ty-ran-no-sore-us) grew to 41ft long and weighed around 8.8 tons, making it one of the largest terrestrial predators ever to walk the Earth. This powerful dinosaur had forward-facing eyes, each bigger than a tennis ball, that gave it excellent binocular vision. This means it could judge depths and distances to objects accurately. However, it was unable to run, only managing a fast walk.

Big, strong neck and shoulder muscles supported the dinosaur's giant head. This grew up to 5ft long, most of which was its mouth which was home to around 60 teeth. The largest were 8in long and were thick like a banana. Coupled with its immensely powerful jaw, *T. rex* would have had one of the strongest bites of any land-based carnivore. It could have crushed bone and ripped more than 110lbs of flesh off in a single bite with ease.

T. rex didn't grind its food down or chop it up by chewing. Instead, it swallowed large chunks of meat whole. Some *T. rex* fossils show bite marks from other tyrannosaurs. Many of these may have come from fights over mates although some were also attempts at cannibalism.

Compared to its huge head, *T. rex*'s arms seem small and puny. While they were too short to reach the creature's mouth, they may have been strong enough to lift loads of up to 440lb. They may have played a role in holding struggling prey still.

TYRANNOSAUROIDS

T. rex was the last of the tyrannosauroids, a group containing many kinds of two-legged meat-eating dinosaurs. One of the earliest of these was *Guanlong* (gwan-long), found in China and living 164-157 million years ago. *Guanlong* was much smaller than *T. rex*, measuring about 10ft long. Its head featured a bony crest on the top that was likely used for display.

Giant Ground Hunters

Some extraordinary prehistoric reptiles called pterosaurs took to the air. These included a group called azhdarchids, some of which grew to incredible sizes. Scientists believe that they hunted on the ground, using their keen eyesight, strong necks, and beaks to dip down and grab small dinosaurs.

ARAMBOURGIANIA 72-66 MYA

Can you imagine a creature with a 6.5ft-long head, a 26ft wingspan and a 10ft-long neck, the same size as a giraffe's? *Arambourgiania* (A-ram-bor-gee-an-ee-a) was that creature. Fossils of this mysterious flying reptile were first found in Jordan. These show its neck to be slim but not very flexible and scientists think despite its great size and giant beak, it hunted on the ground for small prey.

HATZEGOPTERYX 66 MYA

Another extraordinary member of this super-sized family was *Hatzegopteryx* (Hat-zeh-gop-teh-rix). Bulkier than *Arambourgiania* and with a relatively shorter neck, it would have been a formidable sight in the air with its giant, 33ft-wide wingspan. On the ground, the large wings would have been folded up close to the creature's body, allowing this impressive predator to search for prey on all four feet. Because its neck was shorter and thicker than *Arambourgiania*, scientists think that *Hatzegopteryx* may have been able to hunt larger prey, such as young *Telmatosaurus* (Tel-mat-o-saw-rus).

Hatzegopteryx fossils have only been found in a small region of Romania that in the distant past was an island. The absence of other large hunters there may have made this flying reptile the top predator.

Feathered Fiends

Dromaeosaurids (drom-me-oh-saw-rid) were a family of two-legged dinosaurs with feathers. These fierce, agile hunters had a wicked claw on their second toe, a stiff tail, and large, grasping hands.

VELOCIRAPTOR 83-71 mya

One of the most famous of all dinosaurs was actually a lot smaller in real life than in the movies. An adult *Velociraptor* (Vel-oss-ee-rap-tor) was about the size of a large turkey but with a far longer tail and a mouth full of sharp, serrated teeth. Analysis of this hunter's brain showed that it was good at tracking moving prey, a useful trait for an agile hunter chasing after small nimble animals. One amazing fossil preserves a *Velociraptor* fighting a *Protoceratops*, a plant-eating dinosaur about the size of a wild pig.

MICRORAPTOR 125-122 mya

Amongst the smallest of dinosaurs, a fully-grown *Microraptor* (My-crow-rap-tor) stood no higher than your knee and weighed just 2-4lbs. Scientists think it was a glider, but some studies suggest that it might have been capable of powered flight. We do know that the creature preyed on tiny mammals and small prehistoric birds. Some *Microraptor* fossils have been found containing fish scales where its stomach would have been.

AUSTRORAPTOR 78-66 mya

This 16.5ft-long hunter would have towered over most other dromaeosaurid species. *Austroraptor* (Oss-trow-rap-tor) stood almost as tall as an adult human and had a low, slender head, 32in long. Its cone-shaped teeth were well-suited to spearing fish, but it probably also hunted prehistoric mammals and dinosaurs smaller than itself.

UTAHRAPTOR 139-135 mya

Even bigger and bulkier than *Austroraptor*, *Utahraptor* (You-tah-rap-tor) measured more than 20ft long and weighed around 660kg—more than a lion today. Its long arms ended with hands tipped with claws but its most deadly weapon was a large, curved talon on its toe. These could grow to more than 8.5in long and would have been used to pin and grip the dinosaur's prey.

Carnotaurus 71-69 MYA

When José Fernando Bonaparte discovered a new two-legged hunter in Argentina in 1984, he named it *Carnotaurus* (Car-no-tore-us) meaning meat-eating bull. The reason was its pair of thick, short horns on its head just above its eyes—a highly unusual feature for a meat-eating dinosaur. *Carnotaurus* was 24.5 to 26m long and weighed between 2,860 to 4,400lb. This may seem small and light compared to mighty beasts like *T. rex*, but it was its region's biggest and most fearsome hunter.

Carnotaurus had a flexible jaw in its 24in skull. It may have taken quick but not very strong bites out of prey using its 62 teeth. *Carnotaurus* was one of a family of short-faced, two-legged dinosaur hunters called abelisaurids which were the top predators of the Late Cretaceous southern hemisphere. Others include *Majungasaurus* (Ma-jung-a-saw-rus) in Madagascar, *Chenanisaurus* (Chen-an-i-saw-rus) in Africa, and *Rajasaurus* (Raj-a-saw-rus) in India. Evidence shows that *Majungasaurus* was a cannibal.

One of the strangest parts of *Carnotaurus*' body was its arms. They were incredibly small (even smaller than those of *T. rex*) and puny with the lower arm just a quarter of the length of its upper arm. They ended in stubby fingers without claws. This meant that *Carnotaurus*' hands couldn't grasp and grip things. This all suggests that *Carnotaurus* didn't use its arms when hunting at all.

In contrast to its arms, the dinosaur's two legs were strong and muscular. Scientific studies estimate that tail muscles which pulled back the leg each weighed more than 265lb! In fact, much of the dinosaur's weight was taken up with its legs and broad, muscular tail. Paleontologists believe that it could sprint at surprisingly fast speeds for its size - up to 30 miles per hour, more than enough to outrun most prey. It may have struggled with turning sharply though, as its heavy tail probably wasn't flexible enough to balance a sudden, sharp change of direction.

Titanoboa 60-56 MYA

Deep within an ancient tropical rainforest lived a snake of unbelievable dimensions. It could be found lurking within the steaming jungle close to water or hiding beneath the water's surface, ready to strike. The first fossils of this enormous hunter were discovered in 2002 in the coal mines of Cerrejón in Colombia. Researchers couldn't quite believe what they had found—the remains of a snake that could have weighed more than two adult male polar bears.

Titanoboa (Tie-tan-o-bo-ah) was 43-46ft long—the length of a badminton court. It was twice as long as the biggest snakes alive today—the green anaconda and reticulated python. Its body was made up of a huge number of vertebrae bones that formed its spine, perhaps as many as 250. In comparison, a human spine contains 33 vertebrae. At its thickest, midway between its head and tail, the snake had a diameter of 35-39in. Scientists estimate that a full-grown adult may have weighed up to 2,500lb. No other snake gets close to *Titanoboa*'s epic scale.

We now think that *Titanoboa* did its hunting in water or on the fringes of rivers, lakes, and marshes. It wasn't venomous but its powerful muscular body was perfectly adapted to wrap around its prey. It's likely it mostly ate fish but may have dined on crocodiles and turtles that also shared its watery home. Like snakes today, it would have swallowed these meals whole.

GIGANTOPHIS 38-33 MYA

For more than 100 years before the discovery of *Titanoboa*, the largest known prehistoric snake was *Gigantophis* (ji-gan-toe-fiss). Found in northern Africa, it was once thought to be 33ft long but some scientists today estimate its length at 23ft. It was still a formidable beast and may have weighed 1,000lb. Like *Titanoboa*, the snake is thought to have wrapped its powerful body around its prey to crush them.

Meat-Eating Mammals

The very first mammals and their close relatives appeared on land just over 200 million years ago. Some evolved into highly skilled hunters and mammal predators now dominate on land today.

REPENOMAMUS 126-123 MYA

Mammals that lived alongside dinosaurs tended to be small. At roughly 3ft long, the largest species of *Repenomamus* (Re-pe-no-ma-mus) was a relative giant. It walked low to the ground on its short but strong legs and broad feet. It probably preyed on a wide range of creatures including smaller dinosaurs. One fossilized skeleton of a *Repenomamus* unearthed in China contained the bones of a baby *Psittacosaurus* dinosaur in its body where its stomach would be.

PACHYCROCUTA 7-0.2 MYA

Also known as the giant short-faced hyena, *Pachycrocuta* (Pa-kee-crow-coo-ta) stood up to 3.3ft tall at its shoulders. At around 240-285lbs, it may have weighed as much as two adult humans. Its heavy build makes scientists think that it rarely chased prey long distances. Instead, it picked off injured or vulnerable creatures or took over the kills of other animals such as saber-toothed cats.

SIAMOGALE 11-5 MYA

Newly discovered in China in 2017, this giant otter is estimated to have weighed around 110lb—almost twice as much as the biggest otters alive today. Its mouth contained rounded teeth in the cheeks but its jaw was much stronger than large species of otters today. Scientists believe that apart from preying on prehistoric crabs and possibly birds and reptiles, *Siamogale* (si-mo-gale) could have crushed large shellfish between its powerful jaws.

THYLACOLEO 5-0.01 MYA

This large meat-eater roamed the open forests and plains of Australia where it was the largest predatory marsupial. Within its wide and heavy skull lay sharp teeth at the front of its mouth for stabbing and biting prey and large teeth in the cheeks that could slice. *Thylacoleo* (th-i-la-co-lee-oh) also had strong legs that might have helped it climb trees.

South America Terror

For millions of years, before Earth's shifting plates joined it to North America, South America was an island continent. Some unique creatures evolved there, including terrifying mammals and flightless bird hunters.

THYLACOSMILUS 9–3 MYA

At first glance, *Thylacosmilus* (Fy-lac-o-smy-luss) looks like a saber-toothed cat, but this fierce hunter was closely related to marsupials like koalas and kangaroos. Its young were born tiny and under-developed and reared for months in a pouch. As an adult, this leopard-sized creature may have prowled open forest and tree-dotted plains possibly looking to ambush creatures as they munched plants, or scavenge already dead animals. Unlike *Smilodon* (see p26), *Thylacosmilus'* giant, curved canine teeth kept growing throughout its lifetime. By looking at the wear on its fossilized teeth, *Thylacosmilus* is likely to have eaten the flesh but not the bones of its prey.

ANDALGALORNIS 9–6.8 MYA

Andalgalornis (An-dal-gal-or-niss) was a type of flightless prehistoric creature commonly known as a terror bird. The name was well chosen; these birds would have been a frightening sight as they ambushed or chased down prey.

Andalgalornis wasn't the largest terror bird at around 5ft tall, but it was still a formidable opponent. Scientific analysis of the bird's skull shows that it would struggle to shake prey from side to side. In fact, if it attempted that too violently, it might damage its beak. It did, however, have powerful neck muscles and a deadly curved beak that was part of its oversized 14.5in-long skull. Experts believe that it would attack prey like *Diadiaphorus* (Die-ad-dea-for-us)—a sheep-sized plant-eating mammal—out in the open and kill it with sharp, violent pecks.

Pleistocene Predators

Two fearsome meat-eaters lived and sometimes clashed during the Pleistocene Epoch—a recent period of prehistory from 2.58 million to 11,700 years ago. At times, they may have fought over possession of food such as a wounded bison or trapped mammoth.

SMILODON 2.5 MILLION – 10,000 YEARS AGO

These saber-toothed cats roamed the forests and woodlands of North America and parts of South America. Scientists have discovered three species of *Smilodon* (Smie-lo-don) so far. The smallest weighed up to 220lb but the largest, *S. populator,* stood around 47in high and may have weighed more than 950lb; 350lb more than a large tiger today.

It's impossible to ignore this hunter's extraordinary curved canine teeth. These could measure up to 10in long including the tooth root. The cat's jaw had to be able to open very wide to make use of such big weapons. Whilst they would plunge into a creature's flesh, the creature's bite and teeth were rarely strong enough to break through bone.

Smilodon was stocky with a muscular neck and legs. Its relatively short legs were powerful but it couldn't run that fast so probably didn't chase its prey over open plains. Instead, it was most likely an ambush hunter, hiding behind trees and bushes or pouncing on an unsuspecting animal such as a ground sloth, deer, or tapir from a rock or low branch. Experts think that it used its front legs to grapple and hold large prey down, keeping it still long enough to deliver killer bites with its saber teeth.

DIRE WOLF 125,000-9,500 YEARS AGO
Found in North and South America, dire wolves were more muscular than wolves today. They also had bigger skulls, but smaller brains. A dire wolf's jaws were especially strong and possibly used to crush bones to get at the nutritious marrow inside. They may have worked in packs to bring down larger hooved animals as well as scavenged other creatures' kills.

HUNTERS OF THE SKY

Around 230 million years ago, the first animals with backbones took to the air using wings to achieve powered flight. These early fliers were not birds but flying reptiles called pterosaurs and would later share the skies with the first flying birds. Some pterosaurs were enormous with wingspans the size of small planes (see pages 14 and 15). Others were far smaller. *Anurognathus* (An-ur-oh-nay-thus) had a 14-20in wingspan and weighed less than 2 ounces. Looking like a cross between a bat, a bird, and a reptile, this creature hunted insects around 150 million years ago.

Flying Reptiles

Pterosaurs evolved into many different species during the 160 million years they existed. These fascinating creatures developed a range of different hunting techniques.

PTERANODON 86–72 MYA

The crested *Pteranodon* (Teh-ran-oh-don) hunted fish in the ancient seas of what is now North America. Exactly how it hunted is not known, but it may have scanned the water's surface using its good eyesight to spot prey before plunging its beak, or perhaps its whole body, into the water to swallow fish whole.

DIMORPHODON 201–190 MYA

The first *Dimorphodon* (Di-more-fo-don) remains were discovered in 1828 by pioneering female fossil collector Mary Anning. This early flying reptile had a 5ft wide wingspan with broad leathery wings and a stiff tail made up of 30 vertebrae bones. This would have helped balance it as it flew. *Dimorphodon's* over-sized head had a large beak containing two types of teeth, but paleontologists think the force of its bite would have been weak. This did not hamper it from hunting insects and small creatures on land such as reptiles.

PTERODACTYLUS 150.5–148.5 MYA

One of the first pterosaurs ever investigated, *Pterodactylus* (Teh-roe-dack-till-us) was a small flying reptile with a wingspan of up to a yard and weighing up to 9lb. Its long, slender beak was full of small jagged teeth especially at the front. Experts who have studied the wear patterns on its teeth believe that it probably preferred to eat insects and other invertebrates.

PTERODAUSTRO 125–100 MYA

This unusual South America pterosaur boasted a 8ft wingspan and long legs, but its most notable feature was its 12in-long head. Most of its lower jaw was lined with 1,000 bristly teeth with small, lumpy teeth in its upper jaw. Experts think that *Pterodaustro* (Ter-o-dow-strow) may have been a filter feeder. This means it would use the bristly teeth as a sieve to catch shrimp-like crustaceans.

Pterodactylus

Pterodaustro

Prehistoric Birds

Moa were flightless birds native to prehistoric New Zealand that lacked wings altogether. Eating leaves, twigs, and roots, they could grow as tall as 11.5ft and weigh more than 485lb. They faced threat from just one predator, the world's biggest eagle.

HAAST'S EAGLE 2 million to 600 years ago
Haast's eagle had a wingspan as large as 10ft and weighed as much as 35lb—1.5 times more than the heaviest eagles today. Stocky legs ended in powerful talons equipped with 2.5in-long claws. Experts believe the eagle would have launched itself at the Moa's back using its strength to grapple and deliver deadly blows to its victim's neck or skull. It would then eat the Moa's insides. Because there were no other hunters of the Haast eagle's size, it could make a dead Moa last as a food source for many days.

The arrival of human settlers around 800-1,000 years ago spelled the end for both the Moa and Haast's Eagle. The Moa was hunted by humans for food and once it died out, the eagle was deprived of its key food source and was extinct by around 1450.

TIMELINE OF HUNTERS

Life on Earth began around 3.8 billion years ago. Predators have probably been with us for much of that time, existing as microscopic living things in the planet's early oceans. Our timeline begins around 562 million years ago with the current oldest-known and dated fossil of an animal predator called *Auroralumina*.

EARLY PREDATORS

Around 2.7 billion years ago, in Earth's early oceans, a predatory cell engulfed a smaller organism. However, instead of perishing, its prey survived inside it and they formed a partnership (called symbiosis). It was now a new type of cell called a eukaryote (you-ka-ree-oat). Scientists believe these pioneering predators may have evolved into all the animals, plants, and fungi that ever lived.

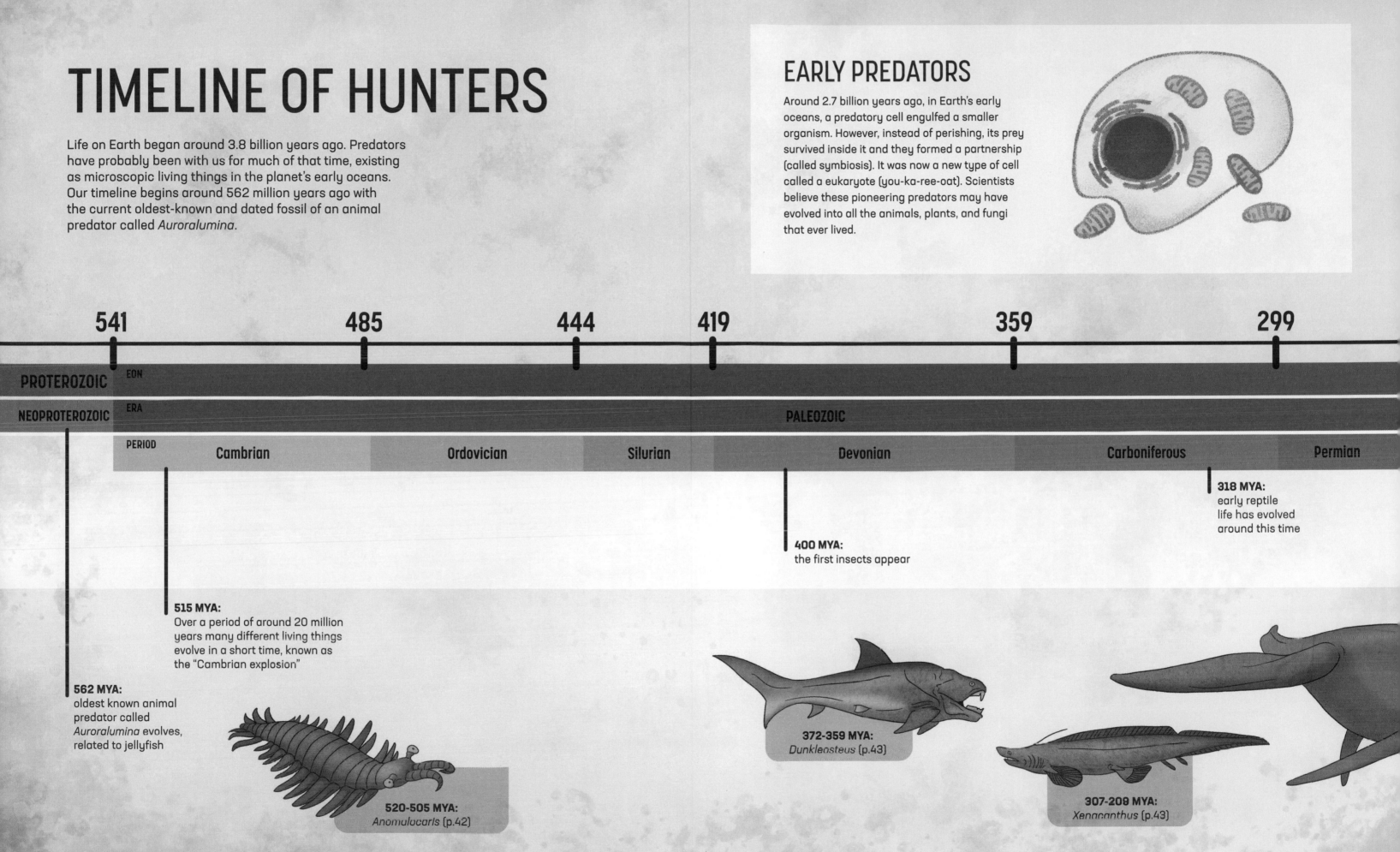

541	485	444	419	359	299

EON PROTEROZOIC

ERA NEOPROTEROZOIC · PALEOZOIC

PERIOD Cambrian · Ordovician · Silurian · Devonian · Carboniferous · Permian

318 MYA:
early reptile life has evolved around this time

400 MYA:
the first insects appear

515 MYA:
Over a period of around 20 million years many different living things evolve in a short time, known as the "Cambrian explosion"

562 MYA:
oldest known animal predator called *Auroralumina* evolves, related to jellyfish

520-505 MYA:
Anomalocaris (p.42)

372-359 MYA:
Dunkleosteus (p.43)

307-208 MYA:
Xenacanthus (p.43)

TERATORNIS 300,000-12,000 years ago

Teratornis was a prehistoric hunting bird that ranged across North America and only died out around 12,000 years ago. With a wingspan of up to 13ft, it must have been an imposing sight. It fed on small prey, swallowing frogs, birds, and reptiles whole but may also have dined out on the carcasses of creatures that had already died.

ELEKTORORNIS 99 MYA

This small creature was an Enantiornithine— a group of toothed, clawed bird-relatives that died out at the same time as the dinosaurs about 66 million years ago. *Elektrornis* (E-lek-tor-or-nis) was small, no bigger than a sparrow, but one part of it was supersized. A leg and foot preserved in amber, found in Myanmar, showed that the bird's third toe was longer than its entire leg. Experts wonder whether it used this to prise insects and grubs out of tree bark.

FEMALE   MALE

Defense Against Attack

Hunters had a wide range of weapons and techniques to secure their food, but what about the creatures that were hunted? Many had their own ways of avoiding attack and trying to survive.

SHEER SIZE

Some plant-eating dinosaurs evolved to truly giant sizes. Four-legged sauropods like *Argentinosaurus* (Ar-jen-teen-oh-sore-us) could weigh up to 88 tons and stand many yards off the ground—simply too big for many hunters to tackle. When young though, these sauropods were much smaller, and were certainly targeted.

SAFETY IN NUMBERS

Some plant-eating dinosaurs, like hadrosaurs, may have lived and moved together in herds. Living in groups meant there was less chance of being selected as prey, and many eyes and ears made it difficult for predators to sneak up unnoticed. Any hadrosaur spotting danger may have signaled an alarm to warn the rest of the herd.

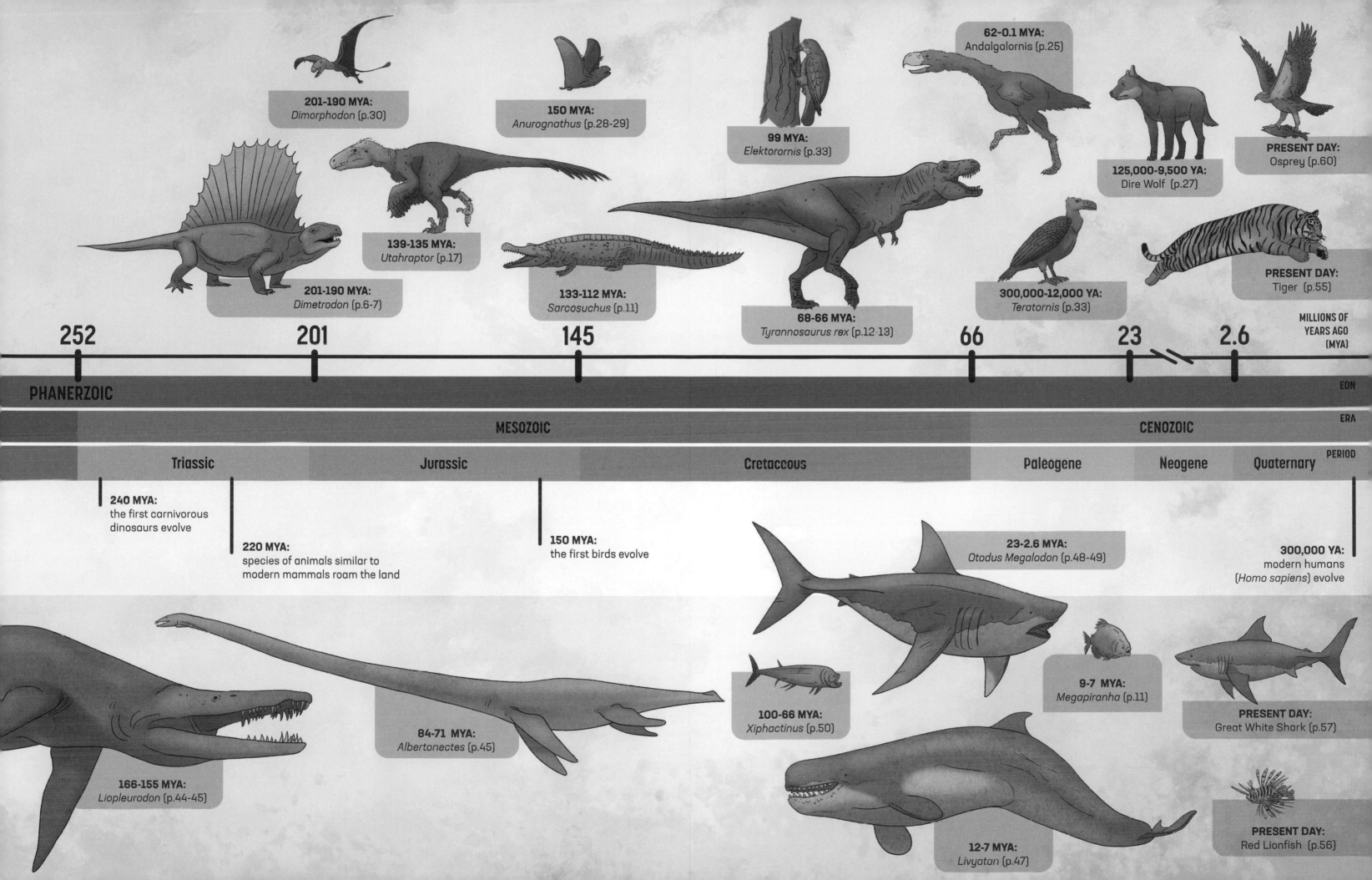

201-190 MYA:
Dimorphodon (p.30)

150 MYA:
Anurognathus (p.28-29)

99 MYA:
Elektorornis (p.33)

62-0.1 MYA:
Andalgalornis (p.25)

PRESENT DAY:
Osprey (p.60)

125,000-9,500 YA:
Dire Wolf (p.27)

139-135 MYA:
Utahraptor (p.17)

133-112 MYA:
Sarcosuchus (p.11)

201-190 MYA:
Dimetrodon (p.6-7)

68-66 MYA:
Tyrannosaurus rex (p.12-13)

300,000-12,000 YA:
Teratornis (p.33)

PRESENT DAY:
Tiger (p.55)

252   **201**   **145**   **66**   **23**   **2.6**   MILLIONS OF YEARS AGO (MYA)

PHANERZOIC   EON

MESOZOIC   **CENOZOIC**   ERA

Triassic   Jurassic   Cretaceous   Paleogene   Neogene   Quaternary   PERIOD

240 MYA:
the first carnivorous
dinosaurs evolve

220 MYA:
species of animals similar to
modern mammals roam the land

150 MYA:
the first birds evolve

23-2.6 MYA:
Otodus Megalodon (p.48-49)

300,000 YA:
modern humans
(*Homo sapiens*) evolve

9-7 MYA:
Megapiranha (p.11)

PRESENT DAY:
Great White Shark (p.57)

100-66 MYA:
Xiphactinus (p.50)

84-71 MYA:
Albertonectes (p.45)

166-155 MYA:
Liopleurodon (p.44-45)

12-7 MYA:
Livyatan (p.47)

PRESENT DAY:
Red Lionfish (p.56)

DEFENSIVE WEAPONS

Some dinosaurs and other prehistoric creatures were heavily armored. *Ankylosaurus* (An-kie-lo-sore-us), for instance, was covered in hard bony plates and knobs that protected most of its upper body from a predator's teeth. It also had a large, heavy clubbed tail which it may have swung like a hammer to strike painful blows at any attacker, or to fight other *Ankylosaurus* for territory or a mate.

CAMOUFLAGE

Just like many animals today, it's likely that prehistoric creatures were camouflaged to make them harder to spot by hunters. Some *trilobites*, for example, were colored speckled brown to disguise themselves on the sea bed. *Psittacosaurus* (Sit-tah-coe-sore-us) was a turkey-sized dinosaur with light shading on the bottom of its body and darker colors on the top. This would have helped it blend in with the forests it lived in around 110 million years ago.

QUICK GETAWAY

Some prehistoric creatures relied on quick reactions to evade attacks. Smaller fish, birds, and dinosaurs were often fast movers. They used their speed to flee at the first sign of attack and get as far away from danger as possible. *Struthiomimus* (Stru-fee-oh-mime-us) was far from small—it was around 13ft long and weighed around 330lb—but its long, muscular legs gave it great sprinting power. Scientists estimate that it could sprint at speeds of 35 miles per hour or more—enough to race away from many prehistoric predators.

HUNTERS OF THE SEAS

The prehistoric seas were alive with dangers for many marine creatures. Terrifying predators lurked in the ocean gloom, ready to strike suddenly and with great force. Even formidable hunters could be hunted themselves. *Thalattosuchus* (Thal-at-oh-sook-us) was one such example from around 165-161 million years ago.

This cousin of today's crocodile had adapted to life at sea with legs more like flippers and special salt glands that helped its body to get rid of the salty seawater. It hunted ammonites, large bony fish, and even pterosaurs that rested on the water. In turn, the 10ft-long predator was threatened and attacked by giant ocean hunters like *Liopleurodon* (Lie-oh-ploor-oh-don) (see page 44-45).

Early Hunters

Life developed in the sea before it evolved elsewhere. Long before dinosaurs arrived on land, the ocean was home to some extraordinary and terrifying predators.

ANOMALOCARIS 520–505 MYA

One of the first hunters, *Anomalorcaris* (A-nom-ah-lo-ca-ris) lived at a time where most marine life was very small. So, at 16in long, it would have dwarfed its victims that it snared with its two front limbs. These were curved and covered in short, sharp spikes for grip. This arthropod's name means "strange shrimp" in Greek, but it wasn't closely related to shrimps at all. It had eyes on the ends of stalks and was covered in overlapping flaps. It moved these to ripple its way through the water. Scientists believe it was a fast and agile predator, capable of catching a range of swimming prey including soft-bodied creatures and sometimes other arthropods.

DUNKLEOSTEUS 372–359 MYA

This formidable fish was huge at up to 13ft long. *Dunkleosteus* (Dun-kel-os-tee-us) was also heavy, weighing around 1.9 tons. That's almost the same as today's great white shark!

Its head was heavily armored with bony plates. Scientists estimate that *Dunkleosteus* may have had the strongest bite of any fish in history. It lacked actual teeth but the plates of its armored jaws acted as sharp blades. Its jaws could shear through bone and shell. This suggests that ammonites and other armored creatures were on its menu.

WEBSTEROPRION 393 MYA

This ancient worm grew to around a yard long but was equipped with vicious half-inch-long jaws. These opened wide to grab unsuspecting fish and other small creatures. Scientists don't yet know if it would have eaten its prey on the spot or, like bobbit worms today, it dragged its victim back into its burrow to devour them.

XENACANTHUS 307–209 MYA

Early hunters also existed in the rivers and other freshwater systems. *Xenacanthus* (Zee-nah-can-thus) was actually a type of shark. It grew up to 6.5ft in length with the rear of its body looking more like an eel. A large spike protruded from its head which may have been venomous and used for defense, while its mouth was crammed full of V-shaped teeth.

Plesiosauria

Plesiosaurs were an extremely successful group of marine reptiles, existing for over 135 million years. The group is often split into two families: the plesiosauroids, which often had long necks and small skulls, and the pliosauroids. The latter included species with huge skulls that generated massive bite forces.

LIOPLEURODON 166–155 MYA

This fierce pliosauroid swam the shallow seas that covered Europe at the time and would have been one of the region's top predators. Its 20-23ft-long stocky, muscular body ended in a large head. Anchored by strong neck muscles, this would have given the creature a supremely powerful bite, allowing its 3in-long teeth to dig deep into large sea creatures.

Liopleurodon (Lie-oh-ploor-oh-don) had four powerful flippers that helped propel it through the water. While scientists don't think it was the fastest hunter in the oceans, a thrust with all four flippers at the same time may have given the pliosaur a sudden burst of acceleration. It may have used this to ambush prey, striking rapidly.

Liopleurodon lacked the gills that fish have so, like all prehistoric marine reptiles, it needed to surface regularly to breathe in air. Like orcas do today, *Liopleurodon* may have chased its prey up to the water's surface, breaching and catching other marine reptiles between its strong jaws.

ALBERTONECTES 84–71 MYA

This plesiosauroid had an incredibly long neck, as long as 23ft, which contained a record-breaking 76 neck vertebrae bones. Its neck was far longer than its body whose muscles moved its four broad flippers. In total, the plesiosaur measured at least 36ft long, possibly longer. Why its neck developed to such great lengths remains a mystery. It may have helped it approach shoals of fish while its large body remained undetected.

Killer Whales

The prehistoric oceans contained a wide range of hunters. Among the largest were two predatory whales that fascinate paleontologists.

BASILOSAURUS 38–33 MYA

When the first fossils of this whale were discovered in the United States, scientists mistakenly thought it was a giant reptile. The ancestors of *Basilosaurus* (Ba-sil-oh-sore-us) had walked on land before returning to the sea and this whale still had traces of its ancestry. The marine giant still had two small hind limbs, no longer present in later whales.

Basilosaurus's 52ft-long body was relatively slender for a whale while its 5ft-long head tapered into a snout. The mouth of *Basilosaurus* contained a mixture of teeth. At the front, they were large and pointed for gripping or biting prey and at the back there were triangular-shaped molar teeth for grinding down food. Scientists estimate that the whale had a phenomenally strong bite force—more than enough to crush bone. *Basilosaurus* would have had no trouble crunching up large bony fish and possibly even bigger prey.

LIVYATAN 12–7 MYA

A ferocious hunter, this large whale could grow up to 59ft long. The first fossils of this creature were discovered in Peru in 2008. Livyatan (Liv-ya-tan) had a giant head, about 10ft long and shaped a lot like the head of a sperm whale. Its mouth was three times the size of the mouth of an orca.

Sperm whales today have lots of small teeth only in their lower jaw. Livyatan's teeth, found in both jaws, were enormous. Some have been discovered that measure over 14in long and 4.5in wide. These are among the biggest teeth found in any hunter's mouth, ever! Scientists have found that the upper and lower sets of teeth sheared past each other when the creature bit down. This could mean that Livyatan was capable of biting and tearing off huge chunks of meat from its prey. We think that it preyed on prehistoric seals and porpoises but would also hunt and attack other whales.

Mega Shark

Few prehistoric sea creatures capture the imagination as much as one enormous shark. First discovered and named in the 19th century, we still don't know everything about this hunter-killer but we do think that it grew to about three times the size of a great white shark.

Otodus megalodon (Oh-toe-dus meg-ah-low-don) lived as far back as 23 million years ago and scientists think it died out around 3.6 million years ago. It would have certainly terrorized other sea creatures. It lived in warm tropical and subtropical waters around the globe as witnessed by its teeth being found on every continent except Antarctica.

A shark's body is mostly gristly cartilage that rots away quickly, meaning it doesn't preserve as well as fossilized bones. A shark's teeth and vertebrae, however, do sometimes survive and scientists build up a picture of a prehistoric shark from the size and scale of these parts. By measuring these we know that it must have reached around 66ft in length and 68 tons in weight. *O. megalodon's* mega teeth were far bigger than any shark alive today.

GIANT TOOTH

O. megalodon's name actually means "giant tooth" and with good reason. Hundreds of its triangular teeth have been found, with the largest being 7in long. This means they dwarf a great white shark's teeth in size (see above). They were far broader too and a single tooth could fill your hand.

O. megalodon had one of the largest sets of jaws ever seen—between 9ft and 11ft wide. The jaws were lined with more than 270 triangular teeth and would have closed with tremendous force, easily capable of crushing bone.

O. megalodon would have taken on large prey, including whales. Unexpectedly, the evolution of a new shark, the modern great white, might have played a role in this giant's extinction. While the extinction of large marine mammals likely contributed to its disappearance, great whites may have also competed against young *O. megalodon* for food.

Monster Mouths

O. megalodon wasn't the only prehistoric hunter with a mouth and weapons that inspire awe, fear, and wonder. Some other sea creatures also evolved with remarkable mouths as well.

XIPHACTINUS 100-66 MYA

This large bony fish had hefty jaws and oversized teeth like fangs. It was at least 13ft long and some *Xiphactinus* (Zif-ack-tih-nus) may have grown even bigger. One fossil found in the US state of Kansas contained an undigested 6.5ft-long *Gillicus* fish—proof that *Xiphactinus* hunted and ate pretty big prey.

MONOSMILUS 45 MYA

Discovered in Pakistan, this cousin of modern day anchovies didn't feed on tiny plankton. It must have hunted other sea creatures judging by its aggressive sets of teeth. It had fangs in its lower jaw and a single curved saber tooth hanging from its upper jaw. It grew to around 3ft in length—six to seven times the size of anchovies living today.

HELICOPRION 290-270 MYA

Fossils of this group of killer fish have been found all over the world. Yet, much about this creature is still unknown. This includes why *Helicoprion* (Hee-lik-o-pry-on) evolved such a weird and dramatic arrangement for its teeth. More than 125 teeth were arranged in a continuous spiral pattern or whorl looking like a deadly circular saw. The lack of scratches on its teeth suggest it ate soft-bodied prey.

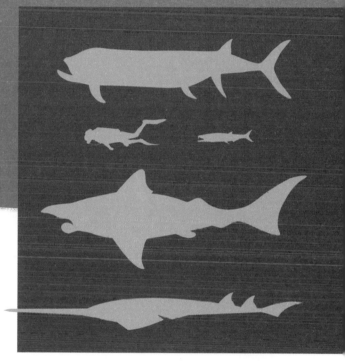

ONCHOPRISTIS 130-70 MYA

This big fish made of cartilage grew up to 13ft long—that's about the length of a motor car. Around a sixth of its length was taken up with its long, flattened snout called a rostrum. This was covered in barbed spikes so that *Onchopristis* (On-ko-priss-tiss) looked a little like a hedge-cutter gardening tool. We don't know if the fish used its rostrum to sense other creatures nearby or whether its spikes were used for hunting or to defend itself. We do know that its mouth contained rows of small, sharp teeth so it may have fed on smaller fishes.

HUNTERS OF TODAY

While dinosaurs, plesiosaurs and saber-toothed cats no longer terrorize other creatures, Earth is still home to many predators. These roam the lands, seas, and skies seeking out prey of different sizes. Many work alone, or like the gray wolf, hunt in packs. A wolf pack typically contains 6-10 members but sometimes more. They track and hunt hooved mammals like deer and elk but will also eat hares, rodents, and waterfowl. Wolves communicate with their distinctive howl that can be heard up to 10 miles away.

Fierce Felines

Among the most majestic of the world's wildlife today are the big cats like the lion, tiger, leopard, and jaguar, all of whom can roar, and the cheetah which cannot. These mammals are some of the most successful and widely distributed predators on Earth. They all have their own hunting strategies, but all are threatened with extinction.

CHEETAH

For sheer pace and acceleration the cheetah is one-of-a-kind. Adults typically weigh just 18-120lb and are really built for speed with a very flexible spine, long legs, and a small, streamlined head. Inside the cat's slender body lies an enlarged heart and lungs which can take up to 150 breaths a minute when sprinting.

A cheetah mostly hunts during the day. It chases down African plains animals like gazelles, springbok, and other antelope using its unrivaled acceleration which can increase its speed in a single stride by 7 miles per hour. They can reach speeds of up to 62 miles per hour, but can only maintain this speed for a short amount of time. Its long tail helps provide balance as it makes swift turns at high speed to catch its prey. When it's not hunting a hooved animal, cheetahs will also catch rabbits and birds.

TIGER

Beautiful but seriously endangered, there are thought to be less than 4,000 of these majestic creatures left in the wild, mostly in India. The largest cats alive today, tigers can weigh 660lb and grow up to 13ft long. Tigers mainly hunt deer and wild boar but will sometimes prey on water buffalo, reptiles, and even porcupines. A single deer can feed a tiger for a week. Tigers are ambush predators, using their stripy appearance to break up their silhouette and sneak up on unsuspecting prey.

JAGUAR

The largest cat in the Americas, jaguars hunt a wide range of creatures—from iguana and tortoises to armadillos, monkeys, fish, and birds. They will fearlessly take on prey bigger than themselves such as tapirs and the predatory caiman, a relative of alligators. Unlike most big cats, jaguars are excellent swimmers and sometimes hunt in rivers. Jaguars have a hugely powerful bite and have even been known to break into tortoise shells.

Ocean Hunters

Just like in the prehistoric past, fish and other marine creatures today need to stay wary in the oceans. Lurking in the waters are some supreme and truly lethal hunters.

RED LIONFISH

This greedy eater may reach 12-16in in length and is protected by an array of 18 venomous spines. It confuses its prey by shooting jets of water at its victim to increase the chances of the fish swimming straight into the predator's mouth.

ANGLERFISH

These deep sea hunters have a fleshy lump on the end of a stalk. They use this as a lure to attract prey toward their mouth which is huge and crammed full of sharp, needle-like teeth. The lure is full of bioluminescent bacteria so it shines brightly in the gloom. Female anglerfish are usually far bigger than males and in some species, the females are as large as a football.

GREAT WHITE SHARK

Sleek and shaped like a torpedo, this shark's powerful tail helps it achieve a top speed in short bursts of 30 miles per hour. Great whites are intelligent and equipped with sharp senses. They can smell one drop of blood in 10 billion drops of water.

They often hunt in different ways depending on their prey. For instance, they will attack seals from below with great speed and force so the shark and its prey both rise up out of the water. A great white shark's mouth is packed full of 300 triangular teeth, some of which grow up to 3in in size. Its bite is powerful and can rip out large chunks of flesh, as much as 33lb at once.

ORCA

Commonly known as killer whales, these are the largest members of the oceanic dolphin family. They are fierce and wily predators, with each hunting pod having Its preferred type of prey. Orcas have been observed beaching themselves on breaking waves to snatch seals on shorelines. Using complex calls, they also work to catch whales, porpoises, and even great white sharks, using their 40-56 teeth which can grow up to 4in long.

Micro Hunters

There are more than a million species of insects, so there's no surprise that they employ a wide variety of hunting and feeding techniques. Some are extraordinary!

BOLAS SPIDER

Instead of spinning traditional webs, these small spiders swing a long thread of silk with a sticky blob of glue on the end. They use it to snare flying moths which they can then draw in rapidly towards their mouthparts.

PRAYING MANTISES

There are many species of mantises but all hunt with terrifying speed and brutality. Their large eyes track prey in 3D before they spring forward using their spine-covered front legs to strike and eat their prey while it's still alive. It's not just insects and spiders on the menu, mantises have been observed hunting lizards, frogs, and small birds such as warblers and hummingbirds.

FEMALE

MALE

3/4in

1/10in

5in

DRAGONFLIES

With a success rate of over 90% every time they go looking for food, dragonflies may be nature's most efficient hunters. A big part of their success is due to their amazing sense of vision. Their huge compound eyes contain thousands of lenses. These give the creature almost 360° vision plus they see more frames of action per second than human eyes. This means they can react incredibly quickly.

Dragonflies are able to make rapid adjustments to their flight and predict where their prey will be in a fraction of a second's time. They usually track their victims from below or behind before catching them in midair. As a result, a large dragonfly can capture and eat its own body weight in flies, midges, butterflies, and other flying insects every day.

ASSASSIN FLIES

There are more than 7,000 species of these flies. Many are lethal. They can catch a bee and other flying insects in mid-flight where they inject their victim with their venom-filled saliva. This kills their prey within seconds and liquefies their insides. The fly is then able to suck the juice up through its mouthparts.

Hunting Birds

Many birds are spectacular and successful hunters. Some use speed, like the peregrine falcon, which when diving down toward prey can reach speeds of over 200 miles per hour. Others use brute force, agility, and timing to snare their food.

OSPREY

While they occasionally snack on reptiles and even crustaceans, the vast majority of this agile bird's diet is made up of fish. Ospreys will fly to 130-165ft above water and then plunge down terrifyingly fast, sometimes reaching 80 miles per hour as they dive in, mostly feet first. The bird has evolved special adaptions for its shallow diving. It can close its nostrils and has see-through third eyelids which it can bring down over its eyes like a pair of swimming goggles. Fish are caught and grasped by its strong talons and feet that grip tightly.

GIANT PETREL

These bloodthirsty seabirds can weigh up to 18lb. They will often follow fishing boats to pounce on any discarded catch, or trapped fish. They even land on top of surfacing whales to take a bite out of them. They scavenge dead seals and penguins and kill other birds that come near their food. They sometimes feast so greedily that they have trouble getting off the ground.

HARPY EAGLES

These powerful eagles glide above the canopy of forests on the hunt for sloths, opossums, and monkeys. Their sharp talons can grow to 5in long and provide a firm grip on their prey which they carry away to feed on. These eagles build massive nests containing more than 300 tree branches and are about the size of a double bed.

SECRETARY BIRD

Despite being a good flyer, this African bird of prey does its hunting on the ground, walking as much as 12-20 miles a day. It is far from a picky eater, consuming almost any small creature that comes across its path from scorpions and lizards to mice and millipedes. It will even tackle venomous snakes such as puff adders. The bird mostly stomps on its prey with a force up to five times its body weight. It then swallows smaller creatures whole. It sometimes uses its beak or feet to break up dung piles on the lookout for insects inside.

Snakes Alive!

There are more than 3,700 species of snake alive today. They range from the Barbados threadsnake which weighs less than half an ounce to giant green anacondas weighing over 440lbs. They hunt in a number of different ways.

Snakes have highly-developed senses and they are sensitive to vibrations made by the movements of other creatures nearby. They have no taste buds but instead use their forked tongue to pick up scents from the air. This information is interpreted by a special organ in their upper jaw. Some snakes including pythons, the emerald pit viper (pictured), and boas have small holes in their faces called pit organs. These can detect the infrared radiation given off by a living animal, meaning that a snake can track warm-blooded prey in dark habitats.

Green Pit Viper

King Cobra

Red Milk Snake

African Rock Python

Spider-tailed Viper

AFRICAN ROCK PYTHON

Africa's largest snake can grow more than 13ft long and weigh over 110lb. It uses its muscular body when hunting, coiling around prey, crushing their victim's body, and stopping it from breathing. Creatures as large as deer, antelope, and warthogs, and even crocodiles are among its prey.

RED MILK SNAKE

This 24-40in-long American snake also crushes its prey like the python, targeting lizards, mice, and other small rodents. Its bright markings though are for self-defense. They mimic highly venomous snakes like the coral snake and trick would-be predators into keeping their distance.

KING COBRA

The longest venomous snake in the world, the king cobra raises its head up to 6.5ft off the ground when threatened. When hunting, it delivers its venom through two sharp, hollow fangs. The effects can be devastating. A single bite can inject more than a teaspoon of venom into prey—enough to kill a dozen people. The snake tends to target other snakes to eat including pythons and kraits.

SPIDER-TAILED VIPER

Living in western Iran, this snake uses its tail as a lure to attract birds. Its tail is shaped uncannily like a spider and the snake moves it to resemble the way spiders move. Many local birds do not fall for this trick but migrating birds passing through fall for it and get close, at which point the snake strikes.

63

Index